*"When we know that we are strong in God's power,
and when we take up the armor He's given to us,
we can stand our ground against the enemy."*

||| | ||||||||| ||||||| || ||| |||
I0145398

Stand Your Ground
By Greg E. Tutwiler

© 2007
Greg Tutwiler

ISBN # 978-0-6151-7935-3

Inquires may be sent to
PO Box 45, Bridgewater, VA 22812
Email to GETutwiler@aol.com

About The Author

*Greg Tutwiler is a Christian Life Coach, Board Certified Pastoral Counselor,
Ordained Minister, member of the American Association of Christian Counselors,
Co-founder of EveryManAlive.com ministries, founder of FreedomLiving.org, and
Publisher of Americana Rhythm Music Magazine.*

Scripture References

Scripture taken from the HOLY BIBLE, NEW INTERNATIONAL VERSION ®. Copyright © 1973, 1978, 1984 by International Bible Society. Use or either trademark requires the permission of International Bible Society.

Scripture taken from the NEW AMERICAN STANDARD BIBLE ®, Copyright © 1960, 1962, 1963, 1968, 1971, 1972, 1973, 1975, 1977, 1995 by the Lockman Foundation. Used by permission.

Table Of Contents

Introduction

"Every man dies; not every man really lives."
William Wallace, Brave Heart

"I have come that they may have life, and have it abundantly."
Jesus Christ (John 10:10)

Are you really living your life to the fullest? Really living the life God meant for you to live? Sadly, many men have been so wounded over the years that we've become a mere glimmer of what God planned for us. And the only way to break the chains that Satan holds so tightly on us is to get our hearts healed and whole. But the battle for our hearts is an all out war. And it's a battle that most do not begin to understand how to enter.

"Without your heart you cannot have God," author John Eldridge writes. "Without your heart you cannot have love. Without your heart you cannot have faith. Without your heart you cannot find the work that you were meant to do. In other words, without your heart you cannot have life." Jesus said in Luke 21:34, "Be careful or your hearts will be weighed down with dissipation, drunkenness and the anxieties of life." It sounds like he knew what we would be up against. It is God's desire to see every man fully restored to the glory He intended; healed and fully alive; living life abundantly.

What would happen if you believed that; if you came to the place where you knew it was true? If you were able to really live the life God intended for you to live? Can you imagine? You could stand your ground when the enemy came, to steal, kill and destroy you.

As I write this, I've just returned from a men's retreat weekend where my brothers in ministry, Dan Grandstaff, Rich Kauffman, and I, presented a message God has put on our hearts. We call it EveryManAlive, and it speaks to men; their hearts; and what God wants to do in their lives.

I've not personally witnessed the power of God move over a group of individuals in the way that He did on this particular weekend. While we knew we had been lead there to minister to these men, we did not anticipate how deeply God would also minister to our hearts.

During one of our times of solitude, I hiked up on a ridge nestled above the retreat lodge located in Highland County, Virginia. On this beautiful sunny day, I sat there reflecting on how awesome God's love for us is. I immediately began to read Scripture, and write in my journal. Eventually I sensed God say, *are you finished yet? Be still, and let me speak.*

Wow! That's so typical though. We feel this need to jump right in and try to make things happen don't we? How can we ever hear that "still small voice," if we fill our time with our own personal clamor?

So I sat, quietly, just breathing. I began to notice the aroma of the forest floor covered with last season's foliage, and the scent of the Creeping Cedar that was growing all around me. In a nearby tree a Woodpecker's quest for lunch echoed across the valley below me. And just above, two Fox Squirrel chased each other up an Oak tree to their nest.

I really don't know how much time passed; ten minutes, maybe thirty. But eventually I sensed God say, *now, open My Word.* And He led me to Hebrews 4:13, which says, "Encourage one another daily, as long as it is called today." That was followed by the message, *don't worry about what others think of you; just serve Me, and let Me bless them through you.*

Only after I had sat quietly, patiently, did He speak directly to my heart. You see, my heart's desire is to encourage others; in fact I believe it's a calling. And my gift from God seems to be the ability to articulate my thoughts through writing. But my vulnerability is inadequacy. Thoughts like 'it's not good enough,' or 'it might be wrong,' or 'what if it sounds stupid?' pop up like land mines all around me when I begin to write.

Yet, I know, beyond doubt, God has things to say through me in this manner. And, He knew I needed confirmation, and release. And that was the gift from Him on that afternoon.

Immediately after God spoke those words of encouragement to me, I felt a wash of warmth come over me, and the words, *now you can go.* "That's it?" I thought. I wanted more. Of course I did. But then, *that's enough,* slipped faintly into my conscious, almost as if from a parting distance. And, of course, it was enough; more than enough. God met me there, affirmed the desire of my heart, comforted my weakness, and sent me down the mountain to be about His business.

So, what you now hold in your hands, I pray, are words of encouragement; from my journey, for your journey; offered to you as they have been given to me. There are 40 short, devotional style stories. Read a one or two at a time, and reflect how they may relate to your life. May God minister to you through these stories as He did to me while they unfolded in my life.

Regaining Control

Any time you begin to deal with issues of the heart, it's painful. And, anytime you begin to regain control of areas in your life that the enemy thought he owned, there will be struggle. It is war. And war is messy. You may be feeling emotionally assaulted. You may feel new or increased tension at work, or in your family. You may feel doubt, anger, shame, or regret. Understand, those feelings are not from God.

Paul said, "Be on guard; stand firm in the faith; be men of courage; be strong. Do everything in love." [I Corinthians 16:13]

Author Bob Gass wrote, "Endurance means staying the course. But endurance is only a word until you have to deal with a strife-torn marriage, the long road back from bankruptcy, divorce or illness, the rebuilding of your life, or the required preparation for success in any field. It takes commitment to keep going when friends fail you, discouragement whispers "give up," and doubt says "it can't be done." That's when endurance takes on new meaning. It becomes your anchor in the storm, your compass in times of confusion, and the head of steam that gets you up the next hill."

Be intentional. A journey means movement. And you have to choose to stay the course. Don't let the workings of the Holy Spirit in your life be like seeds that fall on thorny or rocky ground. You have good soil in your heart. Nurture the seeds of recent healings and revelations. Stay close to God. And don't walk alone. Jesus sent His disciples out two at a time; and He proclaimed "where two or more are gathered in my name ..."

A band of brothers is crucial. We grow from the sharing of our testimony (stories), one to another. We strengthen each other. We encourage each other.

Stand firm. Stay strong. Be men of courage. Fight the good fight. Endure the battle. "Strength and honor," Maximus, in the movie *Gladiator*, said.

So gentlemen; strength and honor!
Stand your ground!

Every Man Alive

There was a tragic story in the news not too long ago about a mountain climber stranded 1,000 feet below the summit of Mt. Everest. The parallels to Christianity were haunting to me. Here's how the headline read; "David Sharp, 34, died apparently of oxygen deficiency while descending from the summit during a solo climb last week." This is the part that really got to me; "More than 40 climbers are thought to have seen him as he lay dying, and almost all continued to the summit without offering assistance." What a tragedy.

One of the climbing parties to happen onto Sharp was that of New Zealander, Mark Inglis. They stopped and found Sharp close to death. "A member of the party tried to give Sharp oxygen, and sent out a radio distress call before continuing to the summit," Inglis said. They just kept on going.

"Several parties reported seeing Sharp in varying states of health and working on his oxygen equipment on the day of his death," the news report went on to say. "I walked past David, but only because there were far more experienced and effective people than myself to help him," Inglis said. "It was a phenomenally extreme environment."

How many times have we found one of our brothers in "various states of declining (spiritual) health," and "walked past" because "it was a phenomenally extreme environment." And we believed that "there were far more experienced and effective people" than us to administer to his needs?

How many of our brothers are "close to death" and we do nothing to help? Satan has mounted a full on assault against us. Men are being taken out all around us. Look at the church (the body of Christ) around you today. How many men do you see living up to their full God potential? How many men lay dieing on their own mountain? Our churches look more like a MASH unit than a platoon ready to take on a fight.

We need to stand together. We need to be available to each other. We need to be ready to stop and help instead of walking on by. And we need to be ready to rally together when one goes down, "low on oxygen and huddled under a rock." It's essential to our survival. We cannot do this alone.

Hillary Tenzing Norgay became one of the first mountaineers to reach Everest's summit in 1953. He said that his expedition "would never, for a moment, have left one of the members, or a group of members, just lie there and die while they plugged on towards the summit."

And that needs to be our attitude. No one left behind to die on "his" mountain. We get through this together with Every Man Alive. That's our rally call. That's our mission. That's our purpose. And that's God's desire.

A New Revolution

On October 31, 1517, Martin Luther nailed his ninety-five theses to the door of Castle Church in Wittenberg. He had enough of the church placing itself between him and God, and I am beginning to get a small sense of how he might have felt.

I know some folks who are watching their denominational church fold up right in front of their eyes. They are having bake sales and yard sales, and special collections to try to pay the bills for the remainder of the year. All the while, they are paying a "good man" $60,000 a year to read half-baked fifteen minute sermons to them once a week. And their bishop has the nerve to chide them for letting their pastor "decline" his cost of living raise.

Driving down the highway the other day, I passed a church with a sign in front of it. It was a big white sign with big red letters; "Jesus Is Coming Soon." I'm sorry, but my thought was 'he better, or there won't be anybody left to come back for.' They would do better with a sign that read "Monster Truck Rally." Sadly, that would get people flooding through their door. And it would probably be more interesting.

Am I the only one here who is getting tired of the way things are? Apparently not, according to author and statistical analyst, George Barna, in his recent book, *Revolution*. "Revolutionaries," as he calls them, "realize that it is not just enough to go with the flow. They are seeking a faith experience that is more robust and awe inspiring, a spiritual journey that prioritizes transformation at every turn, something worthy of the Creator whom their faith reflects. They are embarrassed by language (and actions) that promise Christian love and holiness but turns out to be all sizzle and no substance."

He goes on to say, "In America today, the easiest thing to get away with is going with the flow. The ride is smoother and resistance is minimized." And I have come to realize that the further you maneuver into enemy territory, the more often you're going to get shot at. The more you understand how real the enemy is, and how real the war is that wages around you and against you; the more aware you become of your need to suit up and be in the battle. But of course, that's dangerous. You could get hurt. It's easier to duck and run. It's easier to bail out and leave the battle to someone else. It's easier to "play church" than it is to really get to know God. And of course, $60,000 ineffective preachers, fear tactics, and guilt trips only serve to divide the Body even further.

In Karl Ketcherside's book, *Let My People Go,* he says "The fact is, we are delivering babies who never intend to grow, enrolling students who never intend to graduate, enlisting soldiers who never intend to fight, and registering racers who never intend to run. Our motto has been 'There he is Lord, send him!' The Ship of Zion is no longer manned by a volunteer crew working for sheer love of the Captain, but is steered by a pilot and an assistant pilot, while the remainder are paying passengers who are going along for the ride and complaining as they go."

Your only hope is to trust God and wade deeply into this thing we call Christian faith. The book of Acts (17:10) refer to a sect of people called the Bereans. They "received the Word with great eagerness, examining the Scriptures daily to see whether the things they were taught was so." Too many "believers" aren't even sure what they believe in. We too often let preachers and teachers tell us what to believe without ever going to the one true source for confirmation. "Stand firm," Paul said to the Ephesians. Fight "against the schemes of the devil ... having done everything to stand firm." We must know our God intimately. And we must understand who is against us.

People are counting on us. God is counting on us. This country exists today only because of revolutionaries. Because men, like you and I, stood firm for what they believed in. The Coast Guard has a motto, "So others may live." Jesus died so we could live. And we must fight so our wives and children, and brothers and sisters, can really live. Don't be content to just be a "paying passenger" anymore. William Wallace in the movie *Braveheart* asks, "In your dying day, how many days from that day to this, would you give to have this day back." Let today be the day you choose to step up into the life God is calling you. Let today be the day you say "it ends now!" A friend once said, "It's been a long road in, and it's going to be a long road out." And that's okay. There are plenty of us on that road out, and were picking up hitch hikers just like you at every turn.

Our Wound

"But whenever anyone turns to the Lord, the veil is taken away. Now the Lord is the Spirit, and where the Spirit of the Lord is, there is freedom. And we, who with unveiled faces all reflect the Lords glory, are being transformed into His likeness with ever-increasing glory, which comes from the Lord, who is the Spirit." (II Corinthians 3:16-18)

So many times, and in so many different ways it seems, has this idea of freedom been offered that Jesus puts forth in John 10:10. But so many still struggle under the weight of the battle, and the burden of the wounds we carry. We yearn deeply to savor the life we hear people speak of, yet it eludes us like hunted prey. We want so badly to walk away from the pain, to leave it "in the past where it belongs," but we can't. Steve Stephens in his book, *The Wounded Warrior*, says, "Wounds can make you or break you. It's not the deepness of the wound that kills; it's your refusal to face reality and step forward."

When I read that Scripture, these three ideas speak volumes to me; there is freedom; being transformed; and, with ever increasing glory. We have a promise of Freedom, Transformation, and Glory, if we turn to Christ. We have to give our wounds over to God; that is the only solution. When the wounds surface, and they will, invite Christ into those tender places, and ask Him to embrace those wounds. True healing can only come that way.

Charles Spurgeon wrote, "All that befalls us on our road to heaven is meant to fit us for our journey's end. After all, the Lord gets his best soldiers out of the highlands of affliction."

God has great plans for you. There is more. And it's available now. And probably, for most, it's scary as heck to look at. Or you don't know where to begin looking. Start with prayer; simple prayer. There's no real right way to do this, really. God already knows your heart. He's just waiting for you to take the initiative. Pray, 'God, please show me my wounds; walk me through this; I trust you.' Then spend some time listening. Jot down the things that come to mind. Then begin to pray about those. I think you'll be surprised at what you hear, and at how quickly God will move in.

Bleeding Hearts

"Many a man has died from internal bleeding, and yet there has been no wound whatever to be seen by the eye." (Charles Spurgeon)

I stopped by a local retailer to buy my wife a Valentine gift. We had just returned that day from a wonderful trip together, but I still wanted to honor her with a gift. It was the eve of that big day - the "11th hour - rapidly approaching the, "it's too late now," moment.

I wandered through the floral department, scanning the remains of picked over flowers. There I encountered a rather pitiful fellow; miserable is actually a better word. He was mumbling to himself as he handled the remaining plants with disgust.

Sensing his obvious frustration, a female customer nearby said, "There's a lady clerk over there if you need any help." He looked at me with deep contempt in his eyes and exclaimed, (colorful language withheld) "What do I need to talk to a woman for? I'm already in enough ___ now! I don't need one more woman's opinion about anything!" And he marched off with a small pot of wilted tulips.

Yikes! This guy's got some serious internal bleeding going on. Do you think he even remembers what love feels like? You can only imagine what kind of wounds he's sustained over the past years. They're so deep; he's lost any shred of desire to fight for his heart, let alone that of his wife.

Hopefully you aren't as lost as Mr. Valentine, but you could be; or you could be on the same path. If we don't take up the armor and step into the fight for our hearts, we'll wake up one day, cold, callused, and defeated like this guy; taken completely out of the game. That's the enemy's plan.

John Eldridge says in *Wild At Heart*, "After years of living in a cage, a lion no longer even believes he's a lion; a man no longer believes he's a man."

Get out of your cage. Christ has already broken the lock, we just need to summon the courage to walk out into the open and face the giant head on. Victory is there waiting for the taking.

My Own Pearl Harbor

Have you ever had a day that went from great to rotten in an instant? Days like that make me want to scream. Thankfully they don't happen near as often as they used to; but when it does, it catches me off my guard. Not good.

The most recent one was a doozy. My weekly fellowship lunch was that day, and they're always uplifting and filled with good spiritual food. We closed with an awesome prayer time, and I left there feeling really good about where things in my life were headed. I guess you could say I left the huddle with the ball unprotected. Not good.

Later that night I was trying to locate a computer file with some holiday pictures my family had recently taken. I couldn't find it anywhere. Then the realization hit me that I had probably deleted it accidentally. That was the trigger moment; the sneak attack that opened up a hole in my defenses. It touched off waves of old emotions connected to an experience that's not relevant to this story. But suffice to say, in an instant, my day seemed to crash around me. In that moment, everything good that I had relished in previously that day was now under attack. I was in my own Pearl Harbor with Satan laying down a bombing run like I hadn't experienced in a long time. (And it's understandable now looking back, as I was on the eve of several major stopping points along my spiritual journey.)

Pinned down for hours, I took shot after shot. No vulnerability was left un-assaulted. Fortunately I had the composure and resources to send out a few "cry for help" prayers that at least laid down cover fire until I could mount my counter attack.

By mid-morning the next day the message was coming through that God was calling for a rendezvous with me in His camp. The gentle whisper came; *meet me in the park.* "You're kidding," I thought, it's cold out today. Of course, battle is not limited to only comfortable weather, so then, neither are the encampments. God made the forests. It's His sanctuary. And now he had an aid station waiting for me; and I must go.

As I sat sipping coffee, gazing across the beautiful river, the sun peaked out from a cloud as if God was letting me know He had joined me there. I just sat quietly as He affirmed me and began to restore my heart. Scripture means so much to me, so in that vein, I said aloud, 'can I have a word?' hoping I could leave with something to hang on to. I tried reading passages from several books; Mark, Matthew, James, but there was nothing. I almost put my Bible away thinking maybe I was asking for too much; or trying to make something happen. As I began to close my Bible, I passed by the book of Ecclesiastes. It's one of my favorites, and I almost skipped it anyway because I really didn't want to create the experience.

No, go back, God whispered. And there it was, almost illuminated on the page, Ecclesiastes 3:10-14. King Solomon writes; "I have seen the burden God has laid on men. He has made everything beautiful in its time. He has set eternity in the hearts of men; yet they cannot fathom what God has done from beginning to end. I know there is nothing better for men than to be happy and do good while they live. That everyone may eat and drink, and find satisfaction in all his toil; this is the gift of God. I know that everything God does will endure forever; nothing can be added to it, and nothing taken from it. God does it so that men will revere Him." (NIV)

Immediately I felt restored. The great warrior God, commander-in-chief, had placed his hand on one of His own soldiers and returned him to battle. Everything God does will endure forever. God does this so that men will revere Him. God could have prevented that attack I'm sure. But I sense, looking backward, that I had gotten a little sloppy in my spiritual life. I even now can recall some warning shots that I overlooked. My guard was down.

Have you noticed that sometimes when a sports team is on a winning streak, often times they'll loose what should have been an easy win, right before a major game? And I sense that is what happened to me. And like with those teams, that lose is a wake up call. The big one's coming and you better be ready.

God is so awesome! He knows us so well. And if we'll keep our eyes fixed on Christ, even when we think we've let Him down, He'll come after us with a passion. We're His children, He loves us. He wants us to be happy, and eat, and drink, and enjoy the fruits of our labor. And everything God does will endure forever. Paul tells us to "fight the good fight. Run the race with endurance."

It's not so much about the battles we loose; it's about the war Jesus has already won. In the movie *Miracle*, coach Herb Brooks, drilling his team to exhaustion, said, "do it again." And so, we dust off our coat, get back in the battle, grab our sword, and do it again.

Press On

Those of you who've seen the movie, *Dead Poet Society,* might remember when professor Keating tells the boys huddled in the classroom that their life is an opportunity to "contribute a verse." When you offer a window to others into your life and what God is doing, or what you are battling, you contribute a verse to their journey by sharing your story.

I think the tendency lots of times is to believe you're the only one, or that no one else could possibly be dealing with the same issues you are. We spend much of our time hiding behind ourselves, hoping no one can see into the depth of what's happening on the inside. But when you take a risk and share some of what you are struggling with, or what you have overcome, you give encouragement to the others around you. If the enemy can keep you isolated and pinned down in the quagmire of your struggle, then no one ever realizes that they're not alone.

I found comfort in this from Paul's letter to the Philippians (3:12-14). "Not that I have already obtained all this, or have already been made perfect." That's the beauty of the journey. Too often we're lead to believe that all we have to do is just confess Christ as our savior and everything will change right away. Not so. That's just the rescue. At that point the recovery process begins, and it looks different for each of us. Paul speaks of the journey when he says, "I press on to take hold of that which Christ took hold of me."

He goes on to say, "Brothers, I do not consider myself yet to have taken hold of it. But one thing I do: Forgetting what is behind and straining toward what is ahead, I press on toward the goal to win the prize for which God has called me heavenward in Christ Jesus."

Beware of those who will guilt you into feeling like you're not doing enough to maintain your position in Christ. Paul, who is credited for writing much of the New Testament, tells us that even he was still on his journey. Don't forget, you have been called heavenward. And Paul remarks, "let us live up to what we have already attained."

Your journey really is between you and God. Brothers (and wives and family members) will journey with you, but Jesus wants to restore you to what he has called you to be. All we have to do is "press on," "forget what is behind," and "live up to what we have already attained." There's no time table or duty roster. And remember, you are not alone where you walk. That is where a band of brothers can rally behind each other, and press on together toward the prize, sharing our stories; our battles, and our victories.

Bogged Down and Worn Out

Every year my family vacations for a long weekend over Labor Day with the other members of my extended family. It's something we all look forward to. And it's a chance to get away together from everything that usually occupies so much of our time. I intentionally left my lap top computer at home this year to minimize the distractions. Of course, no one leaves home without our cell phones anymore, so that was firmly attached to my belt clip; ringer off, but power on, "just in case."

We were headed to the mountains, so I lost a signal pretty quickly, but I figured it would return once we reached our destination. Later that evening I checked it again, "just in case" someone had tried to reach me. To my dismay it was dead. No signal, no power, not even a hint of powering up. Not figuring I'd really use it, I had left the charger at home. Suddenly anxiety began to creep in. What if ... ? 'What if what?!' I thought. 'Your whole family is with you, there's no one else that couldn't wait until Tuesday.'

But it bugged me off and on throughout the weekend. I even tried powering it up again once or twice just to make sure I hadn't made a mistake. It wasn't so bad that it ruined my time with my family, but that faint distraction hung with me until I got home and plugged my phone in to see if anyone really had called.

What is that about? We live in an age where "busy" is the most frequent answer when you ask someone how they're doing. We never have any time alone for rest and communion with God. How can we ever expect to hear Him speak when we're so busy?

In most marriages, both adults work away from the home. If we have kids, they are involved in everything; sports, band, youth group, scouts, and social clubs. When they get home from school, if they aren't off to somewhere else, they're nosed up to a computer, chatting and surfing. Mom and Dad are either driving the kids all over the place, or on some social or church committee, or at some meeting, or just too tired. And when we do get to go away, we can't even unplug. We need our cell phones for the ride, and our computers to stay caught up. We don't even talk to the children anymore when we're on the road. We just pop in a DVD, hand them some snacks, and race to our destination. Half the time we need a vacation from our vacation.

We're exhausted and worn out. Most people I encounter today look tired and drained. What happened to that "rest" Jesus speaks about in Matthew, 11:28 "Come to Me, all who are heavy-laden, and I will give you rest." Do you feel heavy-laden? Satan does not want you to rest. He will convince you that you cannot afford to rest. How could you even consider taking a break with all the work you have to do? But you must. If you don't take time to allow Jesus to minister to your heart, you will crash. Your body cannot take the continuous mental pounding dished out from Satan without some spiritual renewal and restoration.

Take time today. Start with just a few minutes in the morning before work, or on your lunch break. Give God a chance to talk to you. Find a quiet, secluded place if you can, and just sit. Don't read or listen to music. Invite God to speak, and then just sit, quietly. You'll be amazed at both the temptation to give up, and the power that God will reveal to you to continue if you just battle through it. Getting alone with God is the key to getting your life back, and it's the key to the peace and rest we so desperately need.

Taken Out

I attended a meeting where a group of men dedicated to the restoration of men's hearts had gathered to hear from one of their own; about how he had fallen deep into the pit of personal destruction. As bad as it sounded, I'm certain that the bottom was still quite a ways down. Afterwards a gentleman spoke for a few minutes, and one statement he made has played over and over in my mind since. "Satan wants every one of us on the front page of the newspaper." (And not in a good way I might add.)

Just the other day my wife commented that all her life, being raised in the church, she always knew the devil was a wicked tempter. "But I've come to realize," she said, "that Satan's goal is to take us completely out of the way." Yes, it is.

Where is the church in all this; sadly, in the line of fire, and in a lot of cases, taken out of the way. Christian men have been cut off, shut down, and rendered, for the most part, ineffective when it comes to living the true life Christ came to offer. And it doesn't just stop with the congregation either. No one is immune, not even leaders. They're even more at risk.

We talk often about how Jesus promises us abundant life. However it is preceded by a warning, and for a good reason. "The thief comes only to kill, steal, and destroy." (John 10:10) In order to have the life that Christ offered, we must understand that we have an adversary who will stop at nothing to prevent us from ever enjoying the life Jesus died for.

Yes, Satan is a tempter, but he's also a deceiver, and a liar. He will tempt you, then convince you that giving into the temptation is okay. He is the Prince of this world. And he has countless weapons at his discretion, all intended to take you completely out of the way.

As men, leaders of the church, our community, and our families; it's time to get real about the threat our enemy poses. We see how horrible the fighting and destruction is in battle fronts like Iraq. We invest soldier's lives, supplies, and major sums of money to defend our beliefs and our allies. And I believe the war for our hearts; our very existence; is equally as fierce; and possibly has even more at stake. Yet we do hardly anything about it.

The guy at the beginning of this story, while not physically dead, has been destroyed. He's down for the count, taken out. Granted, he made the choices that put him where he is. And yes, God can, and will restore a repentant heart. But you can bet Satan celebrates such tragedy. And guys like that go down every day, casualties of the all out war against us.

But as saints, believers in Christ; we are already partakers of the Kingdom of God. We have already been set free. And we have armies of angels on our side, including the great warrior, Christ himself, interceding on our behalf. Don't give Satan ground you've already won. Make your stand, here and now. Mankind needs it's men to take up the fight.

Missing In Action

In the news a while back, rock climber Aron Ralston, while climbing alone, got his arm stuck under an 800 pound bolder. After several days without food or water, and realizing he'd surly die if he waited much longer for help to find him, he amputated his own arm in order to save his life.

Turns out, no one was even looking for him. Aron was known for being gone extended periods of time without any contact. Author Dave Burchett comments; "I would suggest that sometimes our spiritual condition is like that. Others may have no idea how much we are hurt, how desperate the situation, and how trapped we feel because we have withdrawn. Some wounded lambs may be at a life-or-death spiritual point with no help in sight simply because they have not informed their brothers in Christ that they are trapped and desperate."

If you're a hunter, you know that a wounded animal will run off alone to die. Hunters have reported having to track wounded game for a mile or more. Have you ever done that; taken a direct hit, then run off to hide, alone? That is a most dangerous place. Men tend to clam up anyway. We're not big on talk, especially when it gets deep. So there you are, isolated, with a bullet wound through your heart, and no one knows it. And know one's coming to look for you either.

Most times we're too busy with our own lives to realize one of our brothers is spiritually missing in action. Oh maybe, eventually, someone will ask how you're doing, or where you've been; but by then, you've been hiding under that bush for so long, a casual 'doing fine' eeks out in passing, and we move about our day.

You may not be at a place where you need to physically cut off one of your limbs, but sometimes, on the inside, it feels that big. Reaching out to someone you trust and sharing your despair takes guts. And it's a scary thing. I've been there, and felt that 'heart in my throat' anxiety. I've seen the anguish on guys' faces as they open the door to what's really eating away at them inside. But I've also felt the healing power of Christ. And I've seen the life return in men's eyes as the burden lifts from their heart when they bring their pain out in the open.

Psalm 147:3 says God "heals the brokenhearted and binds up their wounds." We don't have to carry that sword around sticking out of our back anymore. God wants to heal our wounds. Maybe you don't know someone directly you can share with, but you can certainly trust God. Don't hang onto those wounds any longer. Let Jesus have them. He knows exactly how to mend them.

Change Hurts

When God has a plan in place, generally there's very little we can do to affect that plan, short of making ourselves miserable trying.

Not long ago I had a job situation change. It needed to change. There were days I wished for it to change. I had invested lots of time and energy into it, but it had become an increasingly frustrating situation.

Isn't it interesting though, when something changes, even though you know it needs to change, we tend to want to fight to hang onto it. I knew I needed to be free of the burden, but thoughts like, "don't I deserve more?", and 'I won't make this easy for you," entered my brain. I knew God had initiated a plan more than two years ago. In fact, I knew God planned to initiate something in my life many years before. (That's another story) But emotions stir and we forget that stuff.

I guess to be honest, I've been aware since I was a young teenager that God was working a plan. But, had you told me then what I would have to go through to be here today, at sixteen I probably would have said, 'no thanks.'

It's been a strange, and at times, quite painful journey. But the joys I have today make it all worth it. The recent situation, while it bruised my ego, was all part of God's plan to get me free enough to enjoy the life that he set within my heart a long time ago; the life I've been searching for.

The enemy wants us to take situations that derail our day and internalize them, stew on them, and fight back. What we may initially perceive to be a negative, often times is God's hand moving across our lives. Change rarely comes without pain or uneasiness. God prunes back our vines in order for them to grow more bountifully, and it hurts. But if we can try to view the changes in our lives from that perspective, often times we will know it is God that's on the move.

As I searched the scriptures that evening for some comfort, I came across this: "This is the Lords doing; it is marvelous in our eyes." (Psalms 118:23) Kind of put it all in perspective I think; marvelous indeed.

Collateral Damage

Two separate experiences last year left me painfully aware of just how delicate the hearts of young children are, and how often adults disregard the importance of protecting that heart.

The first happened on a field trip with my son's 7th grade class. I was in charge of a group of five teenaged boys including my own son. Our group happened upon the aid station where a little boy, probably seven or eight years old, was sobbing and shaking with fear because he had become separated from his mother. My heart broke as I thought how desperate he must feel. A small crowd began to gather, preparing to help the little guy reunite with his mom, when we all noticed a lady charging toward us.

"Where have you been?" she yelled angrily. "You scared the _____ out of me!" Excuse me? Now, this was about her? You could see his poor heart being ripped to shreds. She then proceeded to jerk him up by his shoulders and forcefully place him on a nearby bench where he was commanded not to move until she said he could.

Now, I understand that she was scared, I would have been too. And maybe he's prone to wandering off, and was possibly due some reprimand. I'd be willing to give her that. But at that very moment, your lost son has been found -- alive, unharmed -- rejoice for God's sake. At that moment, he needed a hug. He needed his little heart ministered to. He needed to know he was loved, and that someone cared. And my crew felt his pain. Many were ready to take on the mom right there. I don't blame them.

Not too long after that I witnessed a dad dress down his son, loudly and rudely, in a public restaurant, for what appeared to be only over a minor incident. Everyone in the place turned in his direction. The poor mom looked more like a POW than a loved wife. And Dad proceeded to just stare out the window for the entire meal; except for the occasional "barking" to keep his troops in line, and emotional digs he tossed out. It was all I could do to sit still.

For sure, he's got a gaping hole in his heart, just like the mom in the first story. And that truly is sad. But what happens when we let those wounds lie there untreated; they fester and eat away at us. We turn our pain, anger, discontentment, and fear, into little hand grenades we toss out at our children, wives, family and friends. They explode and rip through someone else's heart, leaving gaping wounds. We leave collateral damage everywhere we go. It's a vicious cycle that gets passed from generation to generation.

But we must make our stand and summon the courage and strength to end it. We must let God heal our hearts so we can stop wounding those around us. My prayer is that if you see any resemblance of yourself in either of these stories, you'll reach out to someone you trust, and share your story. Revisit your wounds. Let Christ fill the void with his healing love. Take back your life from the grips of the enemy. Fight for your heart, so you can fight for your children and your wives.

Shaken Not Stirred

I suppose many of us guys have enjoyed a James Bond flick or two in our lives. He just has that certain charisma about him that makes us want to be that cool. And of course we like all those neat gadgets too. Bond fancies himself a gentleman's gentleman, and drinks those sophisticated martinis. You know, "shaken, not stirred."

That got me thinking as I stumbled across him uttering that famous line on one of my channel surfing expeditions recently. How many of us live lives like James Bond's martinis? How many times has something shaken your life? Maybe you've gotten some really bad news at a doctor's appointment, or you learn your son or daughter has issues with drugs. I'm sure that would shake any of us up pretty good.

What if your doctor tells you that your cholesterol is through the roof and if you continue to eat like you do now, you'll be dead in five to ten years? That would shake me up. But in a couple of days you think to yourself, hey I feel pretty good; nothing hurts, I've got plenty of energy, life's going pretty good right now; and you just casually ignore the warning. Why doesn't that stir us to stop those bad eating habits and do an about face on the way we think about food? Shouldn't it?

When things around you feel like something is just not quite right, or you constantly feel like you're under attack; when it hits the fan almost every evening you come home, and you're in a constant battle with your teenage son; that shakes you, but are you stirred to do something about it?

You see, the enemy doesn't want things to be different. He rather likes you being miserable. When you have a big tiff with your wife, it's like his version of WWF or Smack Down. He's got a front row seat, cheering on every rope dive you dish out. We get "all shook up" of course, but then the moment passes and we breathe a sigh of relief. The Devil convinces us it was her fault anyway, and we just let it pass.

Webster says to stir means, "to move to activity as by pushing, beating or prodding." Don't you think it's time that we allow all this shaking to stir us; to push us to take seriously the warnings, and the attacks, and the disarray we find ourselves in? The apostle John said, "I am writing to you, young men, because you have overcome the evil one." (I John 2:13) He didn't say you can overcome the evil one. As believers in Jesus Christ, you have overcome. It's done. Satan only has the power over your life that you allow. His lies are what keep us from the truth.

Know your position in this Christian life; Paul told the Ephesians, "God has seated us with Him in the Heavenly places." He has "raised us up with Him." We have "boldness and confident access through faith in Him." Now, doesn't that stir you? Satan can't touch that. Whatever shakes you can't touch that. Ask God to soak those truths into your heart. Claim that bold and confident access to the power of your position in Christ. Let God stir that into your life. Believe "you have overcome."

Held Hostage

(William Frey, in *The Dance Of Hope* said, "While we may not know exactly what Jesus had in mind when He promised us life in abundance, we suspect that we haven't found it. And if we identify with any biblical character, it's probably a doubting Thomas, or the man who said to Jesus, I believe; Help my unbelief."

Satan has us so bound up that we can't begin to think outside our own little story. We're held hostage, but it's carefully veiled as "just how life is." What's holding you hostage; keeping you from abundance? Jesus said, "You spend all your energy for food which perishes," (John 6:27). Is it your job, food, money, substance addictions? Maybe its church; being so involved that you don't leave any room for God.

Mine is work. It's so easy to let work related issues take over in my life. If I can finish one more project, answer just one more email, return just one more phone call; then I can call it a day. But it's never really ever all done. There's always a new set of tasks waiting on my desk. And there are plenty of days where I find myself at the end wondering what happened. You can't get that time back either. And Satan loves this part of the day - I think guilt is his favorite dart. Do you know that one?

But Jesus said, "Those who enter the kingdom of heaven have not allowed any earthly concerns to hold them back," (*Words Of Jesus*). We belong to Christ. He will take those burdens from us, but we have to let him. When you are least inclined to pray, (ask for help), that is precisely the right time to do it. Release your earthly concerns to Him. Give Him the busyness and guilt your enemy is assaulting you with, and enjoy the peace His kingdom offers. I have to practice this often, but I know it works. And I know He wants to do the same for everyone. There is an abundance of life just waiting for us if we'll receive it.

Disordered And Confused

Oswald Chambers wrote, "Their faith was real, but it was disordered and confused."

I had a day from down under recently. It was a Tuesday actually; knocked me completely off my feet. Ever had one of those? If it was one thing it was six. And my attitude went straight into the sink. I couldn't shake it, and my faith was on the mat. It wasn't that I doubted God, but as Oswald Chambers put it, my faith was "disordered and confused."

About lunch time, these three words wiggled their way through the muck, *I'm pushing you.* 'Oh come on, not today,' I thought. 'Do we need to do this right now?' Then I went on down to the valley and stewed over it the rest of the day. I tumbled like a barrel over Niagara Falls. I just couldn't shake it.

"We will see ruin and barrenness to know what death to God's blessings means," Chambers continued. "It is certainly not of our own choosing, but God engineers our circumstances to take us there." My wife tried to read this to me before bed that evening "Until we have been through the experience ... then, if we are willing to wait," but I couldn't hear it. I had all the experience I wanted for one day, and wait? Wait for what? A feeble prayer is about all I could muster. That and a good night sleep brought new light and a calmer spirit.

By the following evening a Bible study brought this to me; "Be still and know that I am God." (Psalm 46:10) 'Oh okay, the waiting part.' By Friday, God had revealed to me all of the parts of the bigger picture - his bigger story - for me. I became aware of several other smaller stories that had unfolded simultaneously to bring into reality the plan He was carving out in front of me. I was reminded of a note I had made six weeks earlier, that at the time, was an if/then kind of goal for me personally. The reality was God had orchestrated a when this happens/this will be the situation. He reminded me that a little less than a year ago He called me to take a career risk, in spite of my doubts, and it worked. And then He reminded me that He had been the one who said, "I'm pushing you." Unfortunately my bad attitude had helped me miss the rest. *But I have to take you through the experience - Trust me.*

So the next time circumstances in our life goes south, may we have the composure to get alone with God, listen for His word (all of it), and allow Him to pilot us through the experience. There is a peace within the storm when you know He's in charge.

Return To The Battle

In the movie, *The Patriot*, Benjamin Martin is a colonial freedom fighter who has gathered a band of brothers to take on the Red Coats. Mid-way through the movie he sends his troops - tired and hungry - home for a much needed visit with their families. As they soak in the retreated environment, I suspect many of them questioned their return to the battle. Why wouldn't they?

As Martin awaited their return at the gathering point, you can see the anticipation as he peered through the forest watching for his men to emerge. He would forgive them for sure, knowing himself how hard it was to go back. Yet, one by one, each man, brave, strong, and rejuvenated, returned for the fight. They knew deep down it was a fight worth fighting.

John Eldridge states in *The Way Of The Wild Heart* that, "what I've come to see is that the joy and life God wants to bring us are the things most fiercely opposed. His greatest target is simply your joy."

Stop and think for a moment about that. What is the source of the greatest joy in your life? I find this so true for me. It's where the attack seems to be the most intense. "I always figured his attacks would make most sense around some major evangelistic campaign," Eldridge went on to say; "A mission trip or breakthrough for the church. Nope! This ploy of the enemy is to steal the Father's gifts from us, and so bring us back to the belief we are fundamentally fatherless." And there is where he gets us pinned down and alone, isolated and vulnerable.

We must return to the fight. We must suit up and stand in the face of the enemy. Your joy and your heart is on the line. "Heads up, my brothers. It will be opposed. Let the Warrior rise in you. It's worth fighting for," John said.

Maybe during a season away from the brotherhood you've questioned your return. Why wouldn't you? If you're like the rest of us, Satan doesn't want you to go back. He knows there is strength in numbers. He knows how dangerous you can be; will be, for the Kingdom of God. "What usually happens at this point," John says, "the point when things turn sour, or become suddenly difficult, is that a man just gives up, surrenders the trip, or the relationship, or the dream."

Again we say, let the warrior in you rise up! Pick up your sword and return to the fight with a renewed spirit and resolve to preserve your heart and your joy.

Waking In The Light

One of Satan's greatest weapons against us is isolation. He makes us think we're the only one with a particular issue, or if we tell anyone what's going on with us, then everyone will really know we're not who we say we are.

Well, guess what? If most (or all) of us are thinking that, then we're all in the same boat together. We're really not alone. But it's the fear of the first step, that gut wrenching admission to someone that you need help, or prayer, or someone to confide in, that keeps you in the dark.

In I John, the apostle says, "If we walk in the light;" if we step into our fear and trust God, "As He is in the light;" He meets us there in our pain, "We have fellowship, one with another;" we have brothers we can trust and turn to. This loosens the stranglehold that Satan has on us. And we realize that it's really not us that is being exposed at all; it's the enemy.

We become set free because, "darkness is passing, and the true light is already shining." Isn't that awesome? It's not our fear of exposure at all, it's the enemy's. And by stepping into the light of truth, the darkness in our heart begins to clear away. John goes on to tell us, twice, "You have overcome the evil one."

So when your battle begins to isolate you and heap on the fear and guilt, remember the fellowship of brothers (one with another) that God promises through your faith in His light. Remember Satan's fear of exposure is what's really holding you back. Take that first step, reach out to someone you trust. Expose the enemy for who he really is.

Just To Be Here

"I'm doing good just to be here." Have you ever heard anyone say that? Do you ever feel that way? I'm doing good just to be here. Sometimes I feel like, 'well at least I got out of bed this morning.' Sometimes the attack is so fierce that you wonder if you'll make it out of the desert in one piece. Our enemy wants to destroy us because he knows how dangerous we are. We threaten him.

I heard it said one time that Satan spends our whole lives trying to keep us from ever being saved. And once we are, he spends the rest of our lives trying to make us think we aren't. He loves making us doubt who we are. If he can convince us that we are useless; that we're going to fail anyway so why even try, then we'll walk away from every challenge God lays before us.

Isaiah 40:30-31 says, "Though youths grow weary and tired, and vigorous young men stumble badly, yet those who wait for the Lord will gain new strength." There's that wait word again. Feels more like a weight most of the time, doesn't it? But it goes on to say, "They will mount up with wings like eagles, they will run and not get tired, they will walk and not become weary."

So with the call to wait comes the promise to be lifted up, and made to soar. It doesn't feel like much at the time, but sometimes "just doing good to be here," is actually a victory. Without the promises of God in their hearts, many never get out of bed; many never show up. Many just quit all together.

On those days when all that you can muster is just showing up, understand that you're probably in the heat of major warfare, and showing up is your first move of a counter attack. When you can understand that sometimes just showing up is actually a victory, you will have gone from defense to offence, and taken back ground in the battle for your heart. The pressure begins to ease, and you can begin to see daylight peeking through into your darkness.

It's Not Too Late

John Eldridge sets forth this idea in his book, *Wild At Heart*; "Every man carries a wound … And every wound delivers with it a message." You must understand that. You are not immune. To say, 'I really don't have any wounds, I had a pretty good childhood,' is just denial. They're there, and you must deal with them. We are a world at war, and we need all the men we can get.

In his book, *Bring 'Em Back Alive*, Dave Burchett tells a story that illustrates wonderfully the effect unguarded words have on our hearts. "There was a little boy with a terrible temper. His father gave him a big bag of nails and instructed him to hammer a nail into the fence every time he lost his temper. On the first day the little boy hammered more than three dozen nails into the fence. But as the days went by, the boy began to control his temper more and more. One day the young man realized that he was no longer driving nails into the fence. When he proudly told his father, he was given the new task of pulling out one nail for every day he continued to hold his temper. Finally all of the nails were removed. Then the father took his son out to the fence. 'You have done a great job, son. But look at the holes in the fence. This fence will never be like it was before. When you say things in anger, they leave a scar just like this one. You can stick a knife in a person, but no matter how many times you say I'm sorry, the scar will stay there."

We all have lingering scars, even if they happened long ago. Even though you grew up, moved out, moved on, and put it in your past. Maybe it came from your father, or maybe an older brother, a coach, scout master, teacher, a pastor, or a school mate. Somewhere along the way, someone's words, or actions left a hole, or holes in your heart. Eldridge calls them arrows. And just because you're a Christian, that doesn't make them go away.

But, Eldridge says, "If you are going to know who you truly are as a man, if you are going to find a life worth living, if you are going to love a woman deeply and not pass on your confusion to your children, you simply must get your heart back." Please understand how important that is. Look around you at the youth today. Watch and listen to where they are getting their life instructions from. Why are so many kids smoking, doing drugs, getting pregnant, and taking guns to school?

"We often misunderstand that behavior as adolescent rebellion," Eldridge states, "But those are cries for involvement." Guys, our wives and our children; our churches need us to win this war. The enemy has set us up and we've played right into his game. But it's not too late. Let God take you there. Ask Him to show you where the arrows are. Let Him guide you into those wounds and open them up. Only through the Holy Spirit can healing begin; real healing. Then we can be the warriors, the soldiers, the heroes, the husbands, the dads, that God planned for us to be. And then we can begin to help restore the hearts of those we've wounded.

Join Arms

My son and I like to play this video game where, in co-operative, (together) you must battle through an enemy in order to accomplish a series of tasks. You get pinned down by sniper fire, you get targeted from unseen locations, and you get "taken out," if you don't watch your back. The only way to advance to the next level is if you help each other. You cannot finish the game alone. If your buddy goes down, you get stranded and can't advance until he reemerges restored and ready to back you up.

That to me is a great simulation of life out in our "battle field." When Jesus sent the disciples out to spread the gospel, "he sent them out, two by two." (Mark 6:7). Why; because "Two are better than one." (Ecclesiastes 4:9). We need our comrades in arms, our "Band Of Brothers."

If you are trying to traverse this life journey alone, you'll never advance to the next level. Satan's goal is to keep you pinned down as long as possible. If He can take you out of the game, you can't hurt him, and you can't help anyone else. All too often we'd rather tuck away our pain, guilt, and shame because we don't want anyone to think we can't handle it. We're supposed to be tough. Real men don't cry, right?

I received a letter recently from a business acquaintance. Have you ever felt like this? "I could have died when my appendix ruptured, and no one would have cared, or felt sadness, life would have gone on without me. I didn't make a difference, not even a dent. We only care about ourselves and our survival as individuals. It's survival of the fittest. I figure if nobody cared what happened to me, why should I care anymore."

Don't let yourself get that down. Reach out to a brother you trust. Find a group of men that meet together. Make a friend and join "arms." Jesus said, "For where two or three come together in my name, there I am with them." (Matthew 18:20) When we join forces, we also bring on even more of the power of Christ. Not only can a brother go to battle with you, so will Jesus, we have that promise.

Desire

I love my job. Sure, it has its dull moments and tasks that I'd rather not engage in, but most of the time; it's almost not like work. What I do represents a desire that's been in my heart as long as I can remember. As an editor and publisher of a music related magazine, I get to listen to a lot of different kinds of music, and interact with musicians at various levels of the industry chain. As I write this, I'm attending a music festival in Nashville, TN, featuring song writers. I've heard some fabulous performers; men and women following a dream most of them have had since childhood. Some of them have risked everything to be in this town. It's their hearts desire to make music.

David Whyte writes in, *The Heart Aroused*, "We cannot neglect our inner fire without damaging ourselves in the process." What's your inner fire? What do you long to do before it's too late? Why don't you? Often we live our lives vicariously through that of someone else. Maybe it's a character in your favorite movie; maybe it's a favorite musician, or professional athlete. Maybe it's a neighbor, co-worker, or your own child.

All along, the message playing in your head is that you're not good enough to do that, or you can't afford to take the time to learn a new skill. Or perhaps you're being told you'll surely fail. People will think you're silly, or they might even laugh at you, or ridicule you. The cost becomes too high to take the risk. Moses said to God, "Who am I that I should go ...," and then he proceeded to beg God to send someone else.

God places an "inner fire" in each of our hearts. He calls each of us into something greater than what we've settled for. When you feel that tugging in your heart, don't ignore it. Let God take you there and explore a greater horizon than what you've set for yourself. It's okay to live the life God put us here for. And Jesus said it comes with abundance.

Life, Be In It

Jesus said, "Father, I want those you have given me to be with me where I am." (John 17:24)

Read that again. "I want those you have given me to be with me, where I am." We have been invited into relationship with Christ. That is Jesus' prayer; that we would be with him. It's the enemy that tries to keep you from believing that.

Remember that ad campaign several years ago; "Life, Be In It." God made us to be in life. We are made in his image; "let us make man in our own image," is really what he said. Life is relational. God is relational; Father, Son, and Holy Spirit. He was never alone, and he doesn't want us to be either. If life is all about you; if you think you're the center of the universe; it's not going to work. We're not really in life that way. We're pinned down most of the time, caught in the enemy's cross fire. When he can isolate us from relationships, our effectiveness, and ability to affect people is lost. We're lifeless.

In Lee Cantelon's book, *The Words Of Jesus*, he says, "The message of the one who called himself Messiah is nothing if not confrontational. It Demands a response from those who approach his words. It sounds a revolutionary call to a world that is beset by greed, self-loathing, and denial. It would be safe to say that in Christ's words lies the fundamental essence of change. While there is a comfort and succor in a great many ideas of Jesus, there is also an inescapably radical call that denies us an apathetic response."

Christ's words are the fundamental essence of change and the inescapable radical call up into Him; His story. The choke hold that's on our life, the wounds that are hiding in the caverns of our heart, that battle that keeps us pinned down in our private little fox hole, isolating our hearts from those around us, is demanding a response. Jesus said, "If the Son sets you free, you will be free indeed." He wants to set us free. He wants us to be with Him. He wants us to live; To be in life. Invite Him into those dark places in your heart today and ask Him to take you through them. "Indeed," He says, "you will be free."

The Little Children

I was driving home from work one evening when I passed this young Jedi warrior caught up in a most awesome duel with a rogue fighter. Light saber to light saber, the Jedi stumbled to the ground, certain to be facing his momentary demise. But just as the enemy was about to run him through, the young lad sprung to his feet and caught his foe by complete surprise, dismembering his challenger with one final, and decisive lunge of his glowing saber.

Could you picture it? Did you go there with me, even for a moment? Or did you really see an eight year old boy with a crooked stick in the front yard of his parent's house, dancing around like a kid pumped up on soda and candy bars? I know what he saw. It was reflected in the determined look on his face, and the heroic celebration of the obvious victory dance. He was living an adventure. He won a battle.

What's happened to us? Why can't we be like the little children any more? "Unless you are converted, and become like little children," Jesus said, "you will not enter the kingdom of heaven." Have you lost your since of wonder? Are you too afraid to come out and play? Let that little eight year old boy inside of you out to have some fun. Get caught up in the fairy tales of your life. It's fantastic! The world will tell you to "grow up," "Don't be a cry baby," "Act your age," "Stop acting like a child." but Jesus said, "Unless you become like little children . . " I think he was on to something?

Lovingly And Faithfully Serving

I don't often read the obituaries, but this day was different. A dear man I only knew briefly, passed recently and I was looking for his announcement. A few things struck me as I scanned the page. I noticed the ages of the other folks that died that day: 87, 63, 74, 70, and 34. The last day here on earth is coming for all of us. And for some, when we least expect it. And no matter how hard we may try, there's no escaping it. In Psalms 90:10 we read, "The length of our days is seventy years or eighty, if we have the strength." What are we doing with those precious days of life?

I found the tribute I was looking for. "Lovingly and faithfully served all his life," it said. Yes, he did. Will they say that about you? About me? How will you be remembered when your days are up?

The enemy has us so bound up in the business of life. Most days we get up in the morning, rush to get to work, and mindlessly muddle through the day, just to hurry home, tend to family, and fall into bed, exhausted. How much time can you spend lovingly and faithfully serving like that?

In the SiFi movie, *Alien Vs Predator*, this one line says it all. "We're in the middle of a war, and it's time to choose sides." So, what side are you on? Do you understand that we're in the middle of a spiritual war? You're already in it. If you don't choose Christ, you've already chosen the other side.

Try this. Write your own tribute as if you had lived life the way God wants you to live. Now, live it out. Wake up tomorrow aware that God has a plan for your life. Begin each day asking God for the strength to make that day count. Make "loving and faithfully served" something people will remember about you.

Caring For Your Heart Is An Act Of War

When you enter the battle for your heart, it is an act of obedience towards Jesus. And it's also a declaration of war against the enemy. It is the first move of offensive behavior towards Satan that many of us have ever taken. And he's not happy about it. And he'll do anything to prevent your success.

My job affords me the opportunity to keep odd hours and work from home, thus allowing me the ability to work when I want to (or need to). However this also sets me up at times, because I don't often feel finished. The five o`clock bell doesn't ring in my office. The result is, many days my mind is half at home, half at work. And at times, that keeps me from being completely emotionally available for my kids.

Recently, feeling frustrated about the dilemma, I took a stand against the enemy's assault on my time. At 4:30 pm that day, I turned off the office lights, closed the door, and played all evening with my kids. We played video games, watched TV, played hide and seek, ate ice cream, and read books. They had fun. I had fun. It felt good, and my heart (and theirs) was rewarded immensely.

But as I settled in to bed, my mind began to feel like the battle of Midway. Boom! Instant anxiety over all that hadn't been done landed like torpedoes. The assault bombarded me with thoughts like, "You forgot to ... , you didn't do ... , now that will be late, now you're behind on ... , etc." At some point (about 3:00 am), in the far reaches of my mind I heard, *you're under attack.* Oh yeah, duh. I should have known. "Caring for your heart is an act of war." I knew that. But of course, forgetting it was also part of the attack.

I called in reinforcements (said a prayer for peace) against the onslaught, and eventually drifted off to sleep. When the alarm went off, my memories of the evening before were in tact. God went to war with me, for me, and preserved my obedient efforts with my children. We had gained ground, and advanced the fight for my heart, and theirs.

"Be anxious for nothing," Paul said, "but in everything by prayer and supplication, with thanksgiving, let your requests be made known to God." (Philippians 4:6)

Live For Today

I took a drive one afternoon to the town where I spent the first eight years of my life. I have many good memories from that time in my life. I hadn't been back there in years, and I felt God drawing me there for some reason. I wondered if I would be able to even find my old house.

Sure enough, I drove right there. And it looked just as I remembered it. There was some sense of comfort in knowing that everything was still standing in tact, including the memories; good ones. As I drove away, I wondered if I could find my old school too. I left there in the 3rd grade when my dad got a job transfer. It had been nearly 35 years since I was anywhere near the place.

I found it -- or what was left of it. There it was, in a worn down neighborhood, standing in a jungle of weeds, all boarded up. That contentment earlier in my old neighborhood where I had played cowboys and Indians with my boyhood friends in the woods, ridden bikes and sleds down the old hill, and played baseball at the community field; was gone.

I was saddened by the deterioration. In my mind I could still roam the halls, find the library and cafeteria, and that old stage where my first girlfriend gave me my first kiss on the cheek. I remember playing tag and kickball on the blacktop, now littered with weeds, broken bottles, and bent basketball goals. What a contrast. I paused for a few moments, and then drove off quietly, fighting the tears. "What a shame," my wife said. I couldn't think of anything better to add to that.

Later that afternoon I came across a sign that read, "Cherish the past, anticipate tomorrow, but live today." That's it! I cherish those memories; they are good. And I have hopes and dreams for tomorrow. But today; today is all we can count on. And that day; that day was full of life, even if there were a few tears. That day was lived for the day. And now it too is cherished.

My prayer for you today is that you can rise above all the things that interfere with your life, and live it for today. God provides our daily bread, each day. If yesterday wasn't good, let it go. If tomorrow seems out of control, give it to God in prayer. "Therefore do not worry about tomorrow, for tomorrow will worry about itself." (Matthew 6:34)

Your heavenly Father knows where you are, and what you need. Rest in that truth. "Seek first his kingdom and his righteousness, and all these things will be given to you as well."

A Slurpee And A Prayer

I took my kids out Friday for an evening Slurpee from the local 7-11 store. It's my five year olds favorite drink. He gets a kick out of mixing the flavors, and it's fun to watch his eyes as he anticipates the flavor combination he's chosen. Ah, small blessings!

On this particular evening however, I was left quite frustrated. As we stood in the line to pay for the drink, I noticed what appeared to be a father and daughter in line a few places in front of us. Closer observation revealed a late 30ish something guy, obviously involved with this (16ish) young girl. She walked away for a few minutes and returned with a six pack of wine coolers, and nervously walked out to the sidewalk. The guy proceeded to tell the few of us around him that she "really was 21, just looked young for her age." Right! I was so irritated. And to top it off, the counter clerk, who had witnessed the exchange, sold him the alcohol anyway.

I had so many thoughts running through my head. Call the cops; but I didn't have my cell phone. Confront the clerk; but there were 10 people behind me. Confront the guy; and potentially create a scene. So, as I rationalized what I ought to do, the scene dissipated, and it was too late to do anything.

It bugged me all evening. I have a 16 year old step-daughter who looks about the same age as this young girl did, so it really brought things into perspective. I wanted to rescue that girl. She probably didn't even think anything was wrong with what she was doing. Where were her parents? Where was her dad?

As I settled into bed, I picked up my copy of Oswald Chambers, *My Utmost For His Highest*. This was the quote I read; "The real business of your life as a saved soul is intercessory prayer. Wherever God puts you in circumstances, pray immediately, pray that His atonement may be realized in other lives as it has been in yours. Pray for your friends now! Pray for those with whom you come in contact, now!"

Oh man! I didn't do that. How easy it is to launch out into "what am I going to do now?" I coulda, shoulda prayed. So I did, a bit late, but I did anyway.

"And the Lord turned the captivity of Job when he prayed for his friends." (Job 42:10) "If you are not getting the hundredfold more," Chambers said, "not getting insight into God's word, then start praying for your friends."

Incurable Wounds

Do you ever have days when you feel like this? "Your wounds are incurable. Your injury is beyond healing. You have no one to plead your case. There is no remedy for your wound." (Jeremiah 30:12-13) Sometimes you wonder if you're ever going to make it through this jungle of life.

Jeremiah was describing the hopeless condition of God's people. Yet, just four verses later God declares, "But I will restore you to health and heal your wounds ..." (Vs 17) He has a plan!

David declared in Psalm 119:50, "Your promise preserves my life." The promise is real. And so is the enemy who tries to make you doubt it.

Oswald Chambers said, "Until we get into right relationship to God, it is a case of hanging on by the skin of our teeth." (No wonder my jaw hurts so much!) "Launch out in reckless belief that the redemption is complete, and bother no more about yourself."

On your behalf, Jesus said, "it is finished." Can we not trust the very words of Christ? "I will never leave you or forsake you," he said. We must be like David and receive the promise. We must act on the advice of Chambers and exhibit reckless belief. Until we do, Satan knows we'll live most of our days as if our wounds are incurable. And we all know how effective a wounded soldier is on the battlefield.

Receive not only Christ's death, but rise and ascend into the full authority granted to you through the complete work of Christ. The cross is the door, but the Kingdom is the life. God "raised us up with Him, and seated us with Him in the heavenly places in Christ Jesus." (Ephesians 2:6)

"To be specific, the Gentiles (you and me) are fellow heirs and fellow members of the body, and fellow partakers of the promise in Christ Jesus." (Ephesians 3:6)

We have the promise of life and the power to claim victory of the enemy. Don't be deceived. You are not beyond healing. You are not incurable. There is a remedy for your wound. Christ has gone ahead, on your behalf. Rise from your pain a victorious warrior; a son of God.

Situational Urgency

Last week I was flipping through my check book when I realized the numbers in the register didn't match up to the checks written out. One check in particular, for $900, I was convinced had been written, but was now missing. Then it hit me, I bet I sent it to the wrong place by accident. And if I did, they might not even catch it; deposit it, and then I'd really have a mess. Panic! I spent 20 minutes tearing up my office looking for it. No check. I called the bank, and it hadn't been cashed. Slight relief. I looked some more, retraced my day, then decided it would be best to go to the bank before 2:00 PM and put a stop payment on it just in case. So I dropped everything and rushed out the door.

By the time I reached the bank, I had begun to realize that in fact, I probably hadn't ever actually written the check. I put it in the register, got distracted, and forgot about completing the transaction. Whew! I turned around and drove slowly back home, allowing my heart rate to return to normal.

During my quiet time that evening God reminded me of the situation and challenged me to this: *When was the last time you put that kind of urgent attention and focus on someone, or some situation in prayer?* Ouch! Maybe never? That whole scenario took at least an hour of my day. I was completely centered on resolving the issue. It was real. I was concerned.

But then I thought, I have a 14 year old son, and a 5 year old son. I have a wife. And I have a 16 year old step-daughter, and a 19 year old step-son. Aren't they worth the same amount of time I spent on a missing check? We'll watch a 30 minute sit-com, or a 2 hour movie, or a 3 hour football game; probably multiple times a week. But how often do we spend 30, 60, 90 minutes of focused, dedicated prayer just on one situation or one person?

That missing check was real. The television is real. But so is God. I think sometimes, although we say we believe, we really don't. Not to the point that we believe that investing that amount of time into something in prayer will make a difference. It's easier to try to do it on our own. We'll worry and fret; or we'll take some action based on our own ideas; heck, we'll even spend an hour in counseling. But we won't get alone with God, pour out our heart, read through His word, and then just stay on our knees giving Him time to answer.

How do we ever expect God to come through for us if we don't take the time to invest into our relationship with him? My challenge to you (and me) is the next time you settle down in front of the TV for an hour of mindless entertainment, don't. Instead, take your Bible to a quiet room, and ask God what He would have you do. Pray? Repent? Read? Let Him speak. He will! And your heart will thank you for the effort.

Change Is Painful

Towards the end of Larry Crabb's book, *Finding God*, he deals with the difference between good and bad passions (desires) in our life. He makes this statement, "The measure of what rules us is not which passions feel stronger but rather which passions we are obeying. ... the pleasures of sin are immediately sensual, and they block out pain. The enjoyment of God increases slowly over time, and is regularly accompanied by suffering."

Isn't that true? Why do things that we know aren't good for us still feel good? And when we attempt to do the right thing by God, it's often a struggle. Why do we keep overeating, or smoking, or drinking excessively when we know there's marked health concerns. That big bowl of ice cream tastes so good, even though we know our cholesterol is through the roof.

"Maturing people are sometimes miserable," Crabb adds. Change is painful. Breaking bad habits is tough. Crabb continued, "When bad passions seem to have the upper hand, we must remind ourselves that God is working to entice us with the prospect of knowing Him, and he is appealing to parts of our souls that are not drawn to lesser pleasures. And those parts define who we really are as Christians. God's method of drawing us closer to him is to disrupt the fallen structure by allowing us to feel the terror and pain the fallen structure was designed to overcome. He then entices us with the hope of finding in him the satisfaction of every noble desire."

I've heard people ask, 'why won't God fix that?' or 'I keep praying for God to take away my desire for ___.' God's not going to just fix it. What would we learn from that? But if we tackle the root (the why) of the things in our heart that leads us to pursue things not good for us, then when victory comes; - and it will - we can own that new maturity with conviction. We will know that God pruned a vine in our life, and good fruit will now come forth.

The Thief Comes *(part I)*

Like most folks in this country, my family usually gathers for a evening of food and fellowship in celebration of this country's freedom on the 4th of July. It's always a great time. Cousins, brothers, sisters; and all the littler ones look forward to the games, and conversations, and catching up on family happenings.

This year was like all the rest, with one exception. My oldest son, for whatever reason, had a pocket full of "stuff," including an important storage device for one of his gaming systems. If you know anything about game systems, you understand that as you play most of them, you progress through the game. And the only way you can return to an ending point is to save your progress to a hard drive of some kind each time you play.

As we arrived home from the evening, He discovered the device was missing. "Just great!," he said. "Now I have 20 games that are useless." His evening nose dived in 30 seconds. Just like that, all the memories of the previous five hours were replaced by one minor incident; albeit life changing in his young mind.

The scenario reminded me of times in my life when I allow something to throw me for a loop. In an instant, one event changes your whole outlook on life. Jesus said, "The thief comes only to steal, kill, and destroy." (John 10:10) We must be ever on the lookout for these robbers of our spirit. Do these events present cause for concern? Sure they do. We have to contend with the daily happenings in our lives. But they don't have to steal our focus. They don't have to destroy our progress.

Too often, someone who's dealing with, or has come out of addiction issues, will have a time of progress, only to slip backwards briefly into old patterns. The enemy loves it when this happens. He'll heap on whatever he thinks will defeat you. There we sit convinced we've blown it; right back to square one. Not so. "My sheep listen to my voice," Jesus said. "I know them, and they follow me. I give them eternal life, and they shall never perish; no one can snatch them out of my hand." (John 10:27) We are safe and secure. If the voice we hear sounds anything like guilt, condemnation, or failure, it's not God's.

When life's circumstances seem like they're robbing your "life," step back, and seek understanding before you react. And if it's an issue of sin in your life; "If we confess our sins, he is faithful and just, and will forgive us our sins and purify us from all unrighteousness," (I John 1:9) then deal with it and move on.

Remember, as ransomed individuals, we are merely travelers through this world. We do not have to succumb to its snares. But we must be alert and stand ready.

The Thief Comes *(part II)*

It's amazing how God places examples like the previous story to teach us a lesson. "When life's circumstances seem like they're robbing your life, step back, and seek understanding before you react," was the theme in case you missed it. Apparently I did.

I spent the better part of the next two days wallowing in self pity. I had a series of aggravating events line up over the course of two days that pushed every one of my buttons. I was tanked. I couldn't even take my own advice. I was so frustrated - and defeated. Did I not believe what I had just written? I think that made it even worse. I decided it must be an attack of epic proportions.

Not so fast. By Saturday morning the prayers and pleading for God's intervention seemed to be having an effect. And by the afternoon, clarity was coming through. God revealed to me that what I had perceived as an attack, was really allowed by him to show me some areas in my life that need attention. And as the days progressed, God provided numerous pieces of the solution through various sources.

In my journal I wrote; "my emotions ebb and flow according to the circumstances in my life - and my self worth is often attached to my successes and failures." That's not a good place to be, yet I believe a lot of us camp out there. Oswald Chambers wrote in *My Utmost For His Highest* on July 9th, "We say, If I really could believe! The point is, if I really will believe. No wonder Jesus put so much emphasis on the sin of unbelief. If we really believed that God meant what he said - what should we be like!"

That struck a chord. And so did this; "Even as Christians, we can get so caught up in shaping our own destinies that other options seem unthinkable. We need to be reminded that all our advances, accomplishments, and capacity to affect our future are as nothing compared to the might of God. He really is the one in control," wrote Kimberly Tyree.

My day had been totally out of my control, and I didn't like it one bit. I didn't trust God to see me through either, and my self esteem had been toasted over the whole thing. But on at least two different occasions, God lead me to this passage of Scripture in Psalm 16. There are so many promises nestled in these seven verses, with the key to it all right in the middle.

"Lord, you have assigned me my portion and my cup; you have made my lot secure. The boundary lines have fallen for me in pleasant places; surely I have a delightful inheritance. I will praise the Lord, who counsels me; even at night my heart instructs me. I have set the Lord always before me. Because he is at my right hand, I will not be shaken. Therefore my heart is glad and my tongue rejoices; my body also will rest secure, because you will not abandon me to the grave, nor will you let your Holy One see decay. You have made known to me the path of life; you will fill me with joy in your presence, with eternal pleasures at your right hand." (Psalms 16: 5-11)

Did you catch all of those promises? They are truths we can count on. But the key to it all is, "I have set the Lord always before me." We often call it "getting alone with God," but it's the same thing. It's a daily walking with God. It's prayer, it's devotions, it's worship, it's fellowship; it's intentionally putting God always in front of us, every day. Dallas Willard says if we don't, "it will be simply impossible to find out God's purpose concerning us." And you can bet we'll get the opportunity to learn these lessons over and over again until we get it.

Tomorrow May Never Come

My wife and I love the Outer Banks; specifically Ocracoke Island in North Carolina. It holds special meaning to us, and we cherish the time alone together. It's also a great time of rest and spiritual renewal for me personally. I hear God more clearly there. I'm sure it's as much the down time as it is the location. None the less, I look forward to it all year long.

This year, just like every other time I've been there, we were treated with a most breath taking sunset over the cove known as Silver Lake. It set the tone for the rest of my days there, as I marveled at God's amazing canvas. Minute by minute it changed until the sun faded beyond the horizon, and then it was gone. That particular image will never return. And my photo I took is but a faint glimpse of what was.

That sun rises again each day at home just like it does there. And I've seen some beautiful sunsets at home too, but generally my mind is too cluttered to appreciate them like I do those over Silver Lake. We get so caught up in the daily grind that so much of life passes us by. As I sat on the tranquil ocean shore soaking up more of Gods awesome genius, I journaled this thought; "why do we live our lives like we always have a tomorrow? When it comes to relationships, or important life decisions, or our struggles; why do we put off until tomorrow what we ought to do today?"

Tomorrow is not guaranteed. How many regrets do we want to take with us? Who do you wish you could talk to just one more time before it's too late? Which child do you wish you could make right a situation with? Who needs to know you love them? Who needs to hear I'm sorry?

I had a friend who had a disagreement with her mother. They didn't speak for over a year. She told me how she regretted the separation, and planned to make contact soon. Two weeks later a co-worker found her mother dead in her apartment. My friend's agony over never being able to apologize to her mother was dreadful to witness.

Tomorrow will come, and go, for many of us. And the next day, and the next. But one day it won't. My prayer for you and me is that we'll live each day like it's our last, remembering to make the most of every moment, regardless of where we are, or who we're with. And when the sun sets on another day, the blessing of life, and the opportunity to live it on purpose will bring joy to our hearts, not sadness over regrets, and missed opportunities.

You Get Out What You Put In

We generally don't think it's wise to write a check without money in the bank to cover it. If we do, we can expect the bank to charge us for it. If we're habitual, we can expect to be arrested. You wouldn't go for a long hike without water either. And you wouldn't head out for a long trip without putting gas in your car. There's an order about things. And there's consequences for disregard of the way things work.

This is also true about God. There is a design about the way things work in the Spiritual world around us. Now I'm not talking about following certain rules, or membership requirements, or a specific set of dos and don'ts. That's the stuff of this world. And sadly that's a big part of the problem. But how would we know that?

We have to get ourselves into kingdom thinking. And there's only one way to do that. "If you abide in My word (which means hold fast to the teachings of Christ), you are truly my disciples," Jesus said. [John 8:31] Abide, according to Webster, means to dwell or remain. So that doesn't mean once or twice a week for an hour or so. It means continuously. Anything less is really pointless. In Mark 4:24, it says the measure you give will be the measure that comes back to you. That means you get out of your relationship with God what you put into it. Simple as that. So, how's it going? Are you driving on fumes? Writing bad checks? Hiking without water?

Jesus said, "My kingdom is not of this world. If it were, my servants would fight to prevent my arrest by the Jews. But now my kingdom is from another place." [John 18:36] And we know as believers in Christ, we are also from that other place. "Consequently, you are no longer foreigners and aliens, but fellow citizens with God's people, and members of God's house." [Ephesians 2:19]

We need to get our head up out of the routine of life; the trappings of life; the rules of life; and realize the kingdom life. And the only way to do that is to feed our hearts, minds, and souls with the things of God. Intentional Scripture reading, Prayer, Worship, Fellowship; continuous input from the true source, lead by the Holy Spirit. We need to know who we are, who we belong to, and where we're going. You do not belong to this world in spite of what it tries to tell you. You do not belong to man-made structure. You belong to the Kingdom of God. And that kingdom is where the life is. It's where the freedom is. It's where the peace beyond understanding is. And you can't find it with spiritually "empty bank accounts."

Armor Of God

I woke up at 3:30 AM this morning in a complete panic. I remembered something I had to do today, and began playing out the details in my head. Before I realized it, I was headed into despair over a potential outcome (not likely) several months away.

Then I read this story from Bill Hybel's book, *Who You Are When No One Is Looking*. "The story is told of two prisoners in one small cell with no light except what came through a tiny window three feet above eye level. Both prisoners spent a great deal of time looking at that window. One of them saw the bars-- obvious, ugly, metallic reminders of reality. From day to day he grew increasingly discouraged, bitter, angry, and hopeless. By contrast, the other prisoner looked through the window to the stars beyond. Hope welled up in that prisoner as he began to think of starting a new life in freedom. The prisoners were looking at the same window, but one saw bars while the other saw stars. And the difference in their vision made a huge difference in their lives . . . Vision, like courage and discipline, is a character trait that can be stimulated and developed in anyone who is willing to understand what it really is, and then to work hard at making it part of everyday life. Everyone can choose to look at bars or stars. In fact, everyone makes that choice several times every day."

What I realized is that I was making mental choices to believe a negative thought pattern (a deception) about my day. God gave me that freedom. And instead of recognizing what was driving me into those feelings of helplessness, and choosing to stop it, I ran with it like a fish with bait on a hook. And too many times I'll just go ahead a swallow it, believing the lies being stirred up in my mind. But this time I thought to myself, 'are you mistrusting God again? Are you doubting the promises He made to you? Are you believing a lie being thrust upon you?'

I went straight to my Armor Of God prayer and began to pray it out loud, concentrating on every statement and it's meaning.

The Armor of God
[Adapted from Ephesians 6:10-18]

I am strong in the Lord and in His mighty power.
(Just stop here and think about what that means for a moment.)
Today, I put on the full armor of God so that I can stand against the devil's schemes.
I know my struggle is not against flesh and blood, but against the rulers, against the authorities, against the powers of this dark world, and against the spiritual forces of evil in the heavenly realms.
(No wonder we feel so under attack all the time.)
Therefore, I put on the full armor of God, so that when evil comes, I may be able to stand my ground.
(We can take the enemy on, and win.)
I Stand firm then, with the belt of truth buckled around my waist, with the breastplate of righteousness in place, and my feet fitted with the readiness that comes from the gospel of peace. In addition to all this, I take up the shield of faith, with which I can extinguish all the

flaming arrows of the evil one. I put on the helmet of salvation, and take up the sword of the Spirit, which is the word of God.

And I pray in the Spirit on all occasions with all kinds of prayers and requests. With this in mind, I am always alert, and I keep on praying for myself and for all the saints.

This simple prayer packs so much power. When I pray this, it's like those *Oxy Clean* commercials. The mental dirt dissolves right away. When we know that we are strong in God's power, and we take up the armor He's given to us, we can stand our ground against the enemy. However, we must always be alert, and in prayer in every occasion. And I think therein lies the challenge, and the battle ground for our souls.

Practicing Your Spiritual Swing

A friend shared one of his journal entries recently, and it prompted me to ponder these same questions as they applied to my life. "Why do I always feel somewhat thwarted, and that the enemy has the upper hand? I am often fearful that I will be ruined at any moment if I truly trust. Do you truly love me God? What is it in me that is hesitant about totally releasing everything to you and trusting you? I have a fear about giving all, and being a participant in your larger story to show your glory, if it comes with pain and suffering. There is this thing in me that says I will follow you and trust you, only if you promise safety and no harm. Lord help me to understand these feelings."

My guess is that all of us, if we're honest with ourselves, have similar feelings. For me, it often becomes an issue of faith; of my unfed faith. I have a friend who is an avid golfer. He says he can consistently shoot rounds under par. So I asked him how he was able to play so well. "Practice!" He told me spiritedly. "I spend a lot of time on the driving range and the putting green. You can't just expect to go out cold without any practice and play a good round of golf. You have to practice, practice, practice." That sounded like appropriate advice to me.

So why is it that we can practice our golf swing three or four times a week, and then exercise that training all weekend on a couple of rounds, but we can't seem to even spend a few minutes a day practicing and honing our faith. It's one thing to say we believe in God. Nearly everyone you ask will claim that. But look at what Charles Spurgeon says; "Strong faith, enables the servants of God to look with calm contempt upon their haughty foes." Strong faith brings confidence in the face of the enemy, but it takes practice.

"Above all, we know that the Most High is with us," Spurgeon goes on to say. Do we really know that? When my friend lines up at the Tee shot, he knows he's going to hit a great shot because he's practiced it over and over. And when we practice, and practice, and exercise our faith; faith that has become strong from practice, Jesus stands with us in the face of our enemy with a boldness, and calmness, and confidence only available to those who have invested their time in knowing the ways of the Lord. "When He dresses Himself in arms, where are His enemies? Away then, all fears, the kingdom is safe in the King's hands. Let us shout for joy, for the Lord reigns, and His foes (your foes) shall be as straw for the dunghill."

Do you know that kind of Godly power? You can. And God wants it for you too. Like the worship song "We Will Ride," says, "He has fire in His eyes and a sword in His hand. And He's riding a white horse across this land. And He's calling out to you and me; Will you ride with me?" Will you? Will I? It will take a strong faith, but the victories are so sweet.

What Would Jesus Do?

I know you've seen the bumper stickers and the T-shirts, and all the other items with WWJD on them. And I suppose we all know that it stands for 'what would Jesus do?' Occasionally, when I've found myself in situations where I should "act" a certain way, I would ask myself, 'what would Jesus do?' That's the point of the slogan of course. And at the very least, it would help me think before I acted. But recently I heard someone say, "don't ask what would Jesus do, ask what would Jesus have you do?"

Now, at first glance, you might argue that they really mean the same thing. But look at what Oswald Chambers says. "The one marvelous secret of a holy life lies not in imitating Jesus, but in letting the perfections of Jesus manifest themselves in my mortal flesh ... Sanctification means the impartation of the Holy qualities of Jesus ... It is His patience, His love, His holiness, His faith, His purity, His goodness, that is manifested in and through every sanctified soul. Sanctification is an impartation, not an imitation."

That to me makes more sense. I don't want to copy Jesus, no more than I want to copy Van Gogh if I'm an artist. In fact, the name "Christian" was actually a derogatory term used to mock those that followed Christ. It meant little imitators of Christ. Jesus' manifested qualities in you will most probably look different than they do in me. We're all made differently, for different purposes in God's Kingdom. But the perfected fruits of the Spirit of Jesus are universal; patience, love, holiness, faith, purity, goodness, and the like.

When I write, sometimes it rolls right out, and I look back and think where did that come from? Other times I can't put two sentences together. I sit for hours pouring over one paragraph, then to just delete it and move onto something else. When this happened recently, I contemplated the ideas above. When I thought about what Jesus would do, I came up with multiple scenarios, all of which, at that moment, didn't get to the reason why I was stuck. Then I filtered the situation through the manifested qualities of Jesus; patience, love, holiness, faith, purity .... hmm ... then it hit me like a brick. The thought train hadn't exactly been pure. I was writing with an agenda. I was putting my idea ahead of what God was trying to say. Then God lead me to this verse as way of confirmation. Galatians 3: 1,3 - "Who has bewitched you ... having begun by the Spirit, are you now being perfected by the flesh?" Problem revealed. Of course, I was attempting to do it on my own strength, with my own ideas. It just ain't gonna work that way.

Now don't run over to your office desk and throw out your WWJD pencil caddy. That's not the point here. But I suggest that the next time you're faced with a choice that requires the "right attitude," pass it through the Master filter, and see what comes out on the other side. My guess is that Christ's fruit will wash your fruit, and may even reveal an area at the root of your decision making process that has been affecting you for some time. I don't think just imitating Christ initiates that process. God doesn't want imitators, he wants healed, whole, complete souls. Without applying the Spirit, we're left with incomplete human results. Instead of living from a broken posture, always guarding our actions, we can live from a place of freedom and wholeness, where the manifested Spirit of Christ is as natural through us as breathing. That's what Jesus would have me do.

The Issue Of Motive

The issue of motive has surfaced in multiple ways for me over the past few days. As I've studied through it, I've pushed myself to be more conscious about the motives behind my everyday decisions, and it's been interesting how many times I've re-evaluated some choices as I determined my motive weren't exactly pure.

Look at what Jesus said in Matthew (6:5) about our motives regarding prayer. "And when you pray, do not be like the hypocrites, for they love to pray standing in the synagogues and on the street corners to be seen by men." Peter said, "As obedient children, do not conform to the evil desires you had when you lived in ignorance ... be holy in all that you do." (1:14) These are just two of many examples dealing with motive in Scripture.

Why do you do what you do? As I struggle through a particular job situation that I dislike immensely; I ask, 'why am I staying there?' Financial reasons of course, but is that enough? John Eldridge, in his new audio teaching series, *The Utter Relief Of Holiness*, says "Motive is a really essential category. Why do you check caller ID when the phone rings, and then choose to ignore it. Is it because you're eating dinner and don't want to be disturbed, or is it because you're avoiding a conversation or confrontation that you know will be difficult? Why do you go to church? Is it to really worship God, or is it because you want to be seen as spiritual? Everything we do has a motive behind it."

Oswald Chambers puts it this way, "Jesus says - If you are my disciple, you must be right, not only in your living, but in your motives, in your dreams, and in the recesses of your mind ... No man can make himself pure by obeying laws. Jesus Christ does not give us rules and regulations; His teachings are truths that can only be interpreted by the disposition He puts in us." That means we have the capacity within us to make right decisions from the right motive.

Jay Adams, in his book *Competent To Counsel*, writes, "What makes the difference (in our Christian life) is one's attitude and inner motivation," and he warns against the "attempt to secure a spiritual end by the adoption of habits, the multiplication of rules, and the observance of external standards." Too often we look to institutional structure or personal comfort for our guidelines, and ignore the development of our reliance on the Holy Spirit for help in our decision making. I think deep down, we simply just don't trust God completely with the tough stuff, so we figure we need to do it our own way. More times than I want, I catch myself uttering the words of the father of the boy healed by Jesus in the book of Mark (9:24), "I do believe; help me overcome my unbelief!"

I think it's time we start looking past the "what" we do, and start looking at the "why" we do it. That gets us closer to the core of our soul, and allows us to rely more intentionally on the Holy Spirit for our motivation. If it weren't important, Jesus would not have said, "Blessed are the pure in heart, for they will see God."

Instruments Of Profound Change

In May 2007, I attended a Ransomed Heart boot camp hosted by John Eldridge and his team at Crooked Creek Ranch, outside of Colorado Springs. I know some of you reading this have also been, and you'll probably understand what I'm about to say.

While my friends and I were there, the experience was rich, heavy, deep, and at times painful. Yet it was also an exciting, worshipful, God filled experience. So much happened in our lives personally, and as a team, that it was hard to grasp it all at the time. In the months since though, my journey has been tremendous. As God pulls back the layers of my life, I'm constantly reminded of my time in Colorado. A new kind of revival began in my heart there.

Through that process, I grow more and more aware of just how dire things are in the world today. And my heart's desire increases daily for those around me to experience the same kind of growth, and the same kind of fellowship, and the same rewarding relationship I have with my Father, God. Henry Blackaby writes, "Once you know the truth of God, what you do next is what you believe about God. There is much at stake. Eternity hangs in the balance for man, and you hold the balance. I have never had a time in my life when God has been dealing with me so radically and so thoroughly as now, and I weep before the Lord lest I not come to the level of what He is looking for."

I can so identify with him here. As recently as today, God revealed an area of woundedness that I had dismissed previously. I was hurt, and angry, and enlightened all at the same time. I don't want to go there right now. I don't want to go there again either. But I am also aware that to battle through it will mean significant victory for me in areas of my life that have been debilitating in the past. More importantly, I understand that it factors into what God has planned for me. And any unwillingness on my part here effects others as well. If I don't go there, someone around me may loose an opportunity. What if I hold the balance for many? What if you do? This will take prayer and deliberate intension on my part. It will take greater faith and deeper trust in God too. And of course, that's part of what he's after.

"What is the motivation, or lack of motivation in your life to be a person of prayer," Blackaby continued, "through whom God will change the course of history, or change the course of your family, or your church, or your city or your state or nation. I cannot make that decision for you. God waits to see what you will do next." What will you do next? You have the power to change lives. Are you stalling? Think you can get by without dealing with this one? Do you realize that when God lays an assignment on your heart, he cannot give you another one until you complete the first one? If I won't go there with him; if I won't be faithful with what he asks, he can't take me to the next level. What has he been speaking to you about? "What kind of changes need to be made in your life so that God could work profoundly through your life?" I hope that's your goal. God wants to change your life, and my life, profoundly, so we can be instruments of profound change for others. He's counting on us to come through. Many are.

Fellowship With God

My wife and I had a conversation the other evening about stress, sparked by a class I had taken as part of my biblical counseling training. The instructor offered some interesting insight into how the stress in our lives is actually killing us. "We're burning the candle at both ends these days," he said. And he quoted a study that suggested we need a minimum of nine hours of sleep each night in order for the body to regenerate itself from just the "normal" daily existence. "On average we're two to three hours under-slept." Technology has contributed to the problem by enabling us to extend our daylight into the wee hours of the morning. TVs, computers, cell phones, and even electric lighting contributes to the dilemma.

Heart disease is on the rise. High blood pressure, obesity, anxiety, cases of ADHD and ADD, and heart attacks and strokes are all increasing. We're taking pills for everything. I asked a friend the other day how she was doing; "Busy, busy, busy," she said. "The older I get, the more I seem to take on." Even my mom commented recently, "I think I've got more going on now than when you lived at home. I feel like I'm always on the go." Satan loves the state of the world today. His mission is to burn us out by running us to death, and heap on loads of negative thinking to go along with it. Many of us end up feeling like another friend I heard from recently. "My life has been pretty much the same - work, and pain and misery finding me. I find myself torn between hurt and anger that has me even doubting God's existence." We sure seem to be able to allow time for everything else, accept what's most important, don't we?

Look at what Andrew Murray said. "The first and chief need of our Christian life is, Fellowship with God. It is only in direct, living communication with God that my soul can be strong. The manna of one day was corrupt when the next day came. I must, every day, have a fresh grace from heaven, and I obtain it only in direct waiting upon God himself. Begin each day tarrying before God, and letting him touch you. Take time to meet God. Everything depends upon God taking the chief place."

Can we say that is our daily posture? Man, does this hit home. As I grow, and study, and journey along this path with God, I realize that the days that have been most blessed are those that were the ones spent closest to the Father. And the days I struggled the most are the ones that I stumbled out of bed and fumbled through my day pretending to be the one in charge. How can I ever hope to know God's will for my life if I won't put him at the chief place of my daily life? "In Christ, you are within the veil," Murray said. "You have access into the very heart and love of the father. Bow before God until you get some sense of the greatness and blessedness of the work to be carried on by God in you this day. Say to God, 'Father here I am' ... and wait to hear Him say, 'My child, I give you as much Christ as your heart is open to receive." Think about that for a minute. By aligning ourselves daily with Christ, we are within the veil, in the presence of the Father's love, soaking up all of Christ that we can absorb. Why wouldn't we strive for that every day?

I see the wear and tear of work, pain and misery, and doubting God's existence on way too many faces. It's so unnecessary. It's so not God's plan for us. There's only one solution. Murray concludes, "Begin each day thus in fellowship with God, and God will be all in all to you. As you tarry before God, let it be a deep, quiet faith in Him."

Basking In Sonshine

As I read the headlines today, they seemed to be overly laden with violence. What's new, right? One story in particular though really shook me. It was an execution style killing in New Jersey where four college students were lined up and shot. Why? What would fill someone with so much malice and rage that they would seek revenge like that? Without knowing any other details of that event, my gut feeling is that whoever was responsible, likely didn't even know his father; or worse, was beaten, abused, or completely ignored. None of those are good. You've heard the statistics. I doubt I'm telling you anything you don't already know. But I see way too many of the "bad fruits" out there, and how they act in society, and react to other humans. It disturbs me deeply.

Yet, on the other side; thank God there are men who understand the desperate need for their children to have a dad who steps up to the plate, rolls up his sleeves, and gets into there lives. I attended a wedding this past Saturday where both the father of the groom, and the father of the bride were called on to make a toast to the wedding couple. As I sat there and listened to what these men said, I struggled to fight back the tears, as their words offered to their children reinforced the magnitude of the impact we have on our young ones.

In front of nearly 200 friends and family, the father of the groom spoke with conviction, words of affirmation to his son. "I know no one's perfect, but my son is as close as it gets," he said. "I am so proud of him. He's a wonderful son, and we love him so very much." Oh the look in his son's eyes as he continued to praise him. And then the father of the bride, just as certain, validated his daughter, openly and lovingly. "My daughter was a beautiful baby -- and she is a beautiful woman," he said. "She has been a true blessing to me, and a real joy to raise. She lifts your spirits and makes you feel like you're basking in sunshine." What child doesn't want to hear that from their father? "This is my son, in whom I am well pleased," God the Father told his son Jesus.

Our kids need us dads, desperately. And as this world continues to devolve, they need us even more. They don't need us to be perfect either, they just need us to be real, and available. And we don't need to feel guilty about blowing it in the past. We're not going to get it right all the time. Some of us probably didn't get it right for a long time. But it's never too late to start. I heard a preacher say recently, "occupy the moment." That is so important here. "Never give up," Harriet Beecher Stowe said "for that is just the place and time that the tide will turn."

And turning the tide is what we want. We're in enemy occupied territory here in this world. Satan is at us from all fronts. We must wade into our kid's lives with love, and hope, and understanding, and open arms, and genuine concern for their well being. Never give up dads. Occupy the moment. This is the time and place. Let's turn the tide.

Conclusion

Many of the stories included in this book appeared as a weekly Email devotional style reading called *TrailMix*. If you would like to receive these weekly mailings, email Greg at info@FreedomLiving.org with "Please Add" in the subject line.

You can also inquire about Life Coaching services by sending an email to coaching@FreedomLiving.org.

For more information about EveryManAlive ministries, or to attend an Every Man Alive weekend retreat, write to info@everymanalive.com,
or visit their website at www.everymanalive.com.

Notes and Acknowledgements

John Eldridge, *Wild At Heart* (Nashville, Tennessee, Thomas Nelson, Inc., 2001)

Bob Gass, *The Word For You Today* (Bob Gass Ministries, 2007)

George Barna, *Revolution* (Tyndale House Publishers, Inc., 2005)

Karl Ketcherside, *Let My People Go*
(http://housechurch.org/basics/ketcherside.html)

Dr. Steve Stephens, *The Wounded Warrior,* (Multnomah Publishers, Inc., 2006)

Charles Spurgeon, *Morning By Morning* (Nashville, Tennessee, Thomas Nelson, Inc., 2000)

Charles Spurgeon, *Evening By Evening* (Nashville, Tennessee, Thomas Nelson, Inc., 2000)

William Frey, *The Dance Of Hope* (Colorado Springs, CO, Waterbrook Press, a division of Random House Inc., 2003)

Oswald Chambers, *My Utmost For His Highest* (Uhrichsville, OH, Barbour Publishing, Inc., 1935)

John Eldridge, *The Way Of The Wild Heart* (Nashville, Tennessee, Thomas Nelson, Inc., 2006)

Dave Burchett, *Bring 'Em Back Alive* (Colorado Springs, CO, Waterbrook Press, a division of Random House Inc., 2004)

David Whyte, *The Heart Aroused* (Bantam Doubleday Dell Publishing Group, Inc. 1994)

Lee Cantelon, *The Words Of Jesus* (Creedo House Publishers, 2007)

Larry Crabb, *Finding God* (Grand Rapids, Michigan, 1993)

Bill Hybel, *Who Are You When No One Is Looking* (Inter Varsity Press, 1987)

Jay E. Adams, *Competent To Counsel* (Grand Rapids MI, Zondervan, 1970)

www.ingramcontent.com/pod-product-compliance
Lightning Source LLC
LaVergne TN
LVHW091203080426
835509LV00006B/812